ST. MARY'S
ST. MARY'S CITY, MARYLAND

W9-AQH-233

JESUS
AND THE
REVOLUTIONARIES

HARPER & ROW, PUBLISHERS

NEW YORK, EVANSTON, AND LONDON

1817

42007

JESUS

AND THE

REVOLUTIONARIES

OSCAR CULLMANN

PROFESSOR AT THE UNIVERSITIES OF
BASEL AND PARIS

TRANSLATED FROM THE GERMAN BY
Gareth Putnam

This study is based on my lecture dealing with the same subject, which was given on November 4, 1969, at the Faculté Libre de Théologie Protestante in Paris for the occasion of the beginning of the academic year. It has been, however, substantially expanded for publication.

O.C.

JESUS AND THE REVOLUTIONARIES. *Copyright © 1970 by Oscar Cullmann. All rights reserved. Printed in the United States of America. No part of this book may be used or reproduced in any manner whatsoever without written permission except in the case of brief quotations embodied in critical articles and reviews. For information address Harper & Row, Publishers, Inc., 49 East 33rd Street, New York, N.Y. 10016. Published simultaneously in Canada by Fitzhenry & Whiteside Limited, Toronto.*

FIRST EDITION

LIBRARY OF CONGRESS CATALOG CARD NUMBER: 75-124710

CONTENTS

v

FOREWORD

In all the current discussion regarding the relationship of Jesus of Nazareth to the phenomenon of revolution, the key factor is Jesus' attitude to the situation and movements of *his time*. It is my thesis that Jesus of Nazareth cannot be simply viewed as belonging to any of the principal movements prevailing in his land at his time. For his radical obedience to the will of God, which is anchored in the most intimate communion with God and in the expectation of his kingdom and in his prevailing justice, transcends the framework of those groups which supported the existing order in Palestine as well as those which opposed it with force.

That is not to say that we are setting aside from the start the burning question concerning what Jesus' attitude would be to the indeed related although different "conformist" and "nonconformist" groups of our time. When we, however, concern ourselves *only with the historical question*, it is our intention to show that the problem may not be so simplified as is often done today. The historical investigation will lay the foundation from which we will then be able *correctly* to ask the question to be treated later; namely, how are Jesus' activity and sayings to be made fruitful for our time while remaining faithful to his fundamental attitude, even though the end is no longer expected for the immediate future?

All attempts to confront Jesus with the *present* questions presuppose the answering of the *historical* ones. When we, however, *prematurely* mix the questions and do not endeavor, for the time being, to set aside our modern realities, then we run into the danger firstly of falsifying history and secondly of rendering a poor service to the Christian discussion of current problems by contributing to it an inadequate foundation. That is actually a banality which in former times, when the *eros* for historical truth was more intense, would not have had to be mentioned. Today, however, under the influence of the inappropriate application of philosophical considerations, the endeavor to avoid introducing too hastily our modern circumstances into the historical presentation of Jesus' time has been brought into discredit.

Thus one supports the fatal opinion that anyone, without the least historical endeavor concerning Jesus' attitude, can speak on everyday social and political questions and claim his support for this or that modern solution which one finds personally appealing. One promotes in this way the origin and spread of the unfortunate slogans which distort the historical truth from the start.

I would like in the name of historical truth to request, therefore, that none of my readers, including the nontheologians, reacts at once negatively when he finds attested here and there in the following pages an attitude of Jesus which he rejects in light of modern norms. Only in my concluding remarks will I try to point to some guiding principles in attempting to apply Jesus' attitude to the problems of our time. I hope to be able to convince the reader that this historical detour is worthwhile.

For the third part of this presentation I am naturally forced to some extent to borrow the arguments of my publication, *The State in the New Testament*. They will be placed here in the light of the specific historical question which is to be considered in the entire investigation.

The thesis developed in my previous work concerning the importance of the Zealotist question for Jesus and the understanding of his condemnation has been maintained, since its first appearance in 1956, by a large number of scholars, and indeed naturally also by those who come to conclusions contrary to my own and consider Jesus himself to have been a Zealot or an ally of the Zealots. In view of these one-sided conclusions drawn by those who share my thesis concerning the importance of the Zealot movement for an understanding of the teaching and the life

and death of Jesus, it seems to me especially urgent to supplement my investiga-
tions of *The State in the New Testament*
by showing that, within the framework of
an overall view of the consequences of the
eschatological proclamation of Jesus, those
conclusions not only must not be drawn,
but cannot be drawn.

Basel, January 1970   OSCAR CULLMANN

1 THE PROBLEM

In his *Quest of the Historical Jesus*[1] Albert Schweitzer shows that the entire collection of eighteenth- and nineteenth-century literature written about Jesus' life has distorted the person of Jesus as he actually lived in history, because every author has more or less consciously ascribed to him his own ideas. Thus especially the nineteenth century made of him the representative of certain philosophical, social, and political ideas which were characteristic of this time. Schweitzer indicates in his book the only way to avoid this arbitrary procedure: it involves investigating the life of Jesus in light of the background of thought of *his* time.

Never was it so necessary as today to recall this guidance which is to be drawn from Albert Schweitzer's works, even though such an elementary demand seems so obvious in comparison to current scholarly discussions about hermeneutics. It cannot in fact be overlooked that contemporary theology is once again exposed to the strong influences of the present, partly fashionable way of formulating questions. One thinks, above all, of the prevailing position of sociology in modern thought, which on the one hand can indeed contribute to a clearer and more correct understanding of Jesus' attitude in his time, but which on the other hand leads to the danger of a one-sided, strongly contemporary-oriented characterization of Jesus.

Recently an extremely popular, and in this connection decisive, subject has been that of the relationship of Jesus to the religious and political resistance movement of his time, i.e., to the *Zealots*.

The name "Zealots" is derived from the Greek word *zelos* (zeal), and means the zealous ones, the determined ones, the involved ones (with the nuance of fanaticism). The Zealots at the time of Jesus were zealous for the Jewish Law and cherished a fervent expectation of the imminent dawning of the kingdom of God. How did Jesus conduct himself with respect to this movement? Was he perhaps even himself such a "Zealot"?

Zealotism as a movement within Judaism has been thoroughly examined in a series of recent works. The extensive and important monograph of M. Hengel[2] is primarily to be mentioned. Also I would like to refer to the works of G. Baumbach,[3] who believes that it is necessary to distinguish among the various groups of resistance fighters: on the one hand the *actual Zealots* whose chief demand was a radical reform of the existing temple worship and of the ruling priesthood, and on the other hand the "Sicarii" (a Latin designation literally translated cutthroats, bandits, or assassins) who rather advocated a *political* program with the goal of driving away the Romans and establishing a powerful kingdom of Israel. Faith and politics were, however, *in both groups* extremely closely interwoven, for both groups strived for the overthrow of the existing order and therefore had to fight against the ruling power in Palestine. For this reason one should not overestimate what divided them; we will therefore use the expression "Zealots" to refer, in accordance with the customary terminology today, to all the resistance fighters without wishing to deny the differences which may have existed between them. This terminology is especially justified since the attitude of Jesus to all the Zealots was essentially the same.

As we know, the political-religious revolt led to a real "holy war," the so-called "Jewish War" against the Romans, and to the fall of Jerusalem in A.D. 70. A Zealot group continued the heroic resistance even until the year A.D. 74 in the mountain stronghold of Masada.[4]

The rebellion against the Roman occupation force presented already in the time of Jesus *the* great problem of Palestine, and it was simultaneously a religious and political problem. Romans and Jews had to come to terms with it daily.

The Zealotist agitation, which was in-

creasingly well organized, pressed heavily
like a nightmare upon the Roman officials
in Palestine. They believed themselves to
be threatened from every side by Zealotism.
When the apostle Paul appeared before the
Roman tribune (Acts 21:38), he was asked
whether he was not the Egyptian leader
who had plotted the revolt of the 4,000
"Sicarii" (Assassins), an event which is
mentioned also by the Jewish historian
Josephus. Hence every Jew in New Testament times was forced to take a stand
regarding this problem. It was an especially burning issue since it concerned not
only politics, but also faith and the Messianic hope. The rabbi Gamaliel (Acts 5:36
f.) places Jesus in the same category as the
two Zealot leaders, Theudas and Judas the
Galilean. The violently suppressed insurrection of the latter, which is recorded by
Josephus, was apparently remembered for
a long time.

Today, when one speaks of a "theology
of revolution," the temptation is under-
standably great simply to explain Jesus
himself as a Zealotist resistance fighter.
This view appears at first glance to impose
itself all the more since the teaching and

life of Jesus actually show certain undeniably Zealotist characteristics. In addition, the fact, which is acknowledged by the majority of scholars, namely, that the legal condemnation of Jesus was pronounced by the Romans rather than by the Jews,[5] speaks for such a conclusion. The Romans, indeed, were interested only in the political conduct of their subjects. Among the numerous arguments in favor of Roman responsibility for Jesus' condemnation, the following two should be emphasized: Firstly, Jesus was put to death by crucifixion, the Roman form of capital punishment (the Jewish method was stoning), and secondly, the inscription above the cross, the "titulus," which was probably always posted by the Romans in order to give the grounds of the verdict, named Jesus' striving for kingly rule as his offense,[6] i.e., a political crime which interested only the Romans.

We can understand, therefore, when certain groups today involved in social and political struggles against the existing order, within and outside the Church, readily refer to Jesus as a "revolutionary." We can understand it even better since there have for a long time been scholars who, independent of tendencies determined by prevailing moods, have viewed Jesus as a Zealot or at least an ally of the Zealots. This is true for H. S. Reimarus,[7] later for K. Kautsky[8] and R. Eisler,[9] and most recently for the well-known English New Testament scholar, S. G. F. Brandon,[10] who goes a long way in the direction described above.

We will concern ourselves above all with the argumentation of the above-mentioned scholars without, however, referring to each one of them when their arguments are in agreement with each other. It seems to us, on the other hand, of little avail to dwell on an investigation of certain more recent sensation-oriented publications, which are written by less competent authors and utilized then for demagogic purposes through the use of well-known slogans.

First of all we must establish that the relevant sayings and narratives of Jesus in the Gospels may be divided into two groups: those representing him as closely connected with Zealotry, and those seeing him on the contrary set apart from it. It is thus easily understood that accordingly as one relies *exclusively* on the first or *exclusively* on the second, Jesus can be set forth on the one hand as a revolutionary or on the other as a decided opponent of every resistance, indeed actually as a defender of the existing order.

Do we have the right, however, to consider only the one group of sayings and narratives or the other? We will see that both, one as well as the other, are rooted in the life and teaching of Jesus. Consider to begin with the characteristics which *closely connect* Jesus with the Zealots: Jesus, as well as the Zealots, proclaimed that the kingdom of God is at hand.—Jesus was conscious of fulfilling a decisive divine mission in the establishment of this kingdom.—He was critical of Herod, whom he called a "fox" (Luke 13:32).—He spoke ironically of the kings who rule over the people and oppress them by the use of force while adorning themselves with the title of "benefactors" (Luke 22:25).— Certain of his sayings concern the carrying of weapons.—Then there is what pertains to the life and activity of Jesus: e.g., his influence on the crowd who according to John 6:15 wanted to make him king, and the power of attraction which he had over the Zealots (among the Twelve there was at least one, Simon the Zealot,[11] who was a member of a Zealot group before he became one of Jesus' disciples.[12] I have shown elsewhere that this was possibly also true of others, perhaps of Peter "Barjona,"[13] and most probably of Judas Iscariot, whose surname "Iscariot" could very well contain the designation "Sicarius").[14] —Furthermore, the cleansing of the temple, the entrance into Jerusalem according to the circumstances reported by the Gospels, and the carrying of weapons by one or several disciples in Gethsemane were able to be interpreted, although unjustifiably, already in the time of Jesus as Zealotist acts. —Finally, and of great importance, there is the already mentioned fact that Jesus, as the inscription over the cross shows, was condemned by the Romans as a Zealotist agitator.[15]

The opposing arguments, which on the other hand set Jesus forth precisely as an opponent of every political resistance and every act of violence, are just as forceful and numerous: There are all the sayings advocating nonviolence (not to resist evil, etc., Matt. 5:39 ff.).—There is the exhortation to love our enemies, the Beatitude concerning the peacemakers, and the command not to draw the sword.—Then there is Jesus' fundamental faithfulness to the Law.[16]—Further, there is the fact that Jesus took in a tax collector among the Twelve and that he had social contact at all with tax collectors, the representatives of the occupation force.—Above all, however, Jesus' energetic repudiation of any political elements in the divine mission, which resulted in his viewing Zealotism as *the* great diabolical temptation, is to be mentioned.

It is clear that the proponents of the thesis that Jesus was a revolutionary, and those of the thesis that he was, on the contrary, a defender of the existing order, must exclude either the one or the other group of sayings and narratives of Jesus. There is a very simple means for accomplishing this: One suppresses those which contradict the thesis which one supports himself. Anyone, however, who seriously concerns himself with the exegesis of the Gospels is forced to explain the existence of those elements in the Gospels which stand in the way of the view that he defends. Even so, however, a completely acknowledged scientific method of exegesis of the New Testament suggests a procedure which, if it is *uncritically applied,* would be equally simplistic and arbitrary. In this case it is asserted that only the sayings which support one of the alternative theses were really spoken by Jesus, whereas those which express the contrary were first subsequently attributed to Jesus by the believing community. Hence only the one group of occurrences is considered historical, and the others are seen as a conscious or unconscious creation of the early Christian community ("community-formation").[17]

One assigns all too often today the role of scapegoat, so to speak, to the believing community, a role which once was ascribed to Paul by viewing him as the one who distorted the gospel of Jesus. Now it is not at all my intention to discredit in principle that duty which is incumbent upon every serious exegete, and which, as form criticism teaches us, consists in considering the role of the community in the formation of the Gospels. Rather I am opposing exclusively the *arbitrary,* naïve, unrestrained application of a method which is in and of itself legitimate. It is simply not justifiable, with the help of this method (distinguishing between authentic words of Jesus and "community-formations"), to push aside all that speaks against one of our favorite assertions. The exegete should impose upon himself in this respect an extremely strict self-discipline.

Furthermore, the proponents of both theses, who take into consideration *only* the one or *only* the other set of texts, commit an initial error which is fatal to their treatment of the problem. They proceed from the *a priori* that Jesus' attitude must be *simple*: either he was a revolutionary or he was a defender of existing institutions. one does not reckon at all with the possibility that Jesus' attitude toward worldly institutions, without being contradictory, *had* to be complex, because his thinking proceeded entirely from his expectation of the end. Whereas oversimplifications, in accordance with the French expression *terribles simplificateurs*, are "terrible" in all areas, they are especially so when applied to Jesus. Jesus' double attitude to an unjust world, whose end he proclaimed and *within* which his disciples must now work for a kingdom that is not of this world, is neither contradictory nor a compromise. Both sets of sayings and narratives of Jesus with which we are concerned derive from the same source: Jesus' central future hope, his *expectation* of the coming kingdom.[18] That is the common origin.

Albert Schweitzer has also shown us the way here when he, in order to warn us against modernized distorted views of Jesus, stresses the necessity of regarding this expectation of the coming kingdom as the key to the entire teaching and activity of Jesus. If we take his direction seriously, then it follows for our problem that for Jesus all the realities of this world were necessarily *relativized* and that his allegiance, therefore, had to lie beyond the alternatives of "existing order" or "revolution." In contrast to the Zealots Jesus proclaimed that the kingdom of God comes from God and that its realization is not dependent upon us. The parable of the secretly growing seed (Mark 4:25 ff.) points to this conviction.

Here it is especially important to practice the self-discipline of which we have spoken and which should lead us to set aside the ideas and conceptions which we are especially fond of today. The fear of the slogan, "Religion—the opiate of the masses," should not induce us to try to understand the teaching of Jesus *apart*

13

from the eschatological perspective of the coming kingdom. Furthermore, the expectation of the coming kingdom, which is not of this world, does in no way detain Jesus from his work *in* this transitory world and *for* this transitory world. On the contrary, it is an incentive for this work, especially since his *norms* were not taken from this world, which God will bring to an end. True Christian eschatology does not favor in any way passivity, inaction, or "immobilism."

On the basis of this eschatological perspective we are able to understand the double attitude of Jesus: (1) to the temple worship existing during his time, (2) to the social order and especially (3) to the institution of the state. The eschatological perspective binds these three problems together; indeed, they comprise one single problem. We will only theoretically differentiate them in the following presentation. For ultimately the questions of worship and of the social order flow into the political one, as can be concluded from Jesus' death, the crucifixion by the Roman authorities. The attitude of Jesus to the temple as well as his sayings concerning social injustice *had* to bring him sooner or later into conflict with the political authorities, whose task was the maintenance of order and to whom every national movement appeared suspicious. The question of resistance to the state must occupy us accordingly somewhat longer. First, however, we will turn to the questions of worship and of the social proclamation.

2 THE QUESTION OF WORSHIP

Jesus cleansed the temple. This event seems most clearly to speak in favor of the thesis "Jesus—Revolutionary," and it also is always placed in the foreground by the proponents of this thesis. Does not such a striking act constitute the point of departure and the criterion by which all the other elements of the gospel tradition can and must be judged? In any case this event must be an obstacle to the advocates of the contrary one-sided thesis "Jesus—Defender of the existing order." Is this event, however, also an obstacle to the thesis which I am seeking to defend here, namely, that Jesus, while radically and uncompromisingly opposing injustices, stood beyond the frequently cited antitheses in his relationship to the existing institutions?

I will resist the temptation to grasp the all too simple solution of contesting the historicity of the cleansing of the temple event. Even so, serious exegetes have suggested this solution out of objective and purely historical reasons. Thus M. Goguel tends to the view that the early Church constructed this narrative from a simple verbal protest of Jesus against the buying and selling in the temple.[1] E. Lohmeyer[2] and (according to D. Fr. Strauss,[3] who himself, however, accepts a historical core), Origen also question the historicity of this scene. It is asserted that the temple police and the Roman garrison would have had to intervene against such an act. Further, it is suggested as unthinkable for such an event not to have been brought up as a point of accusation in the trial proceedings against Jesus. According to others, in any case, the act which Jesus performed does not deserve the importance which is attributed to it. At the most peace and quiet were momentarily disturbed.

Nor are there sufficient reasons either to deny the event of the cleansing of the temple or to belittle it.[4] However, it should not be placed into a false perspective. It may be called "revolutionary," but was it really a Zealotist act?[5] This assertion contains nevertheless a kernel of truth: the Zealots, like the Qumran sect, aspired, as we have seen, radically to reform the temple cult and the existing priesthood. But first of all the Zealots wanted to destroy the existing organization by the use of force; secondly, they wished to set up another within the earthly framework. Both of these aspects are missing in the case of Jesus. In cleansing the temple he undoubtedly attacked an important component of the sacrificial system, and certainly defied the priesthood by doing it. But he definitely did not have in mind the double goal pursued by the Zealots, the overthrow of the entire temple and priestly organization and the replacement of it by another.[6] Openly he proclaimed in the manner of the prophets the destruction of the temple: "There

will not be left here one stone upon another" (Mark 13:2*). And in front of the
high priest the destruction of the temple
was mentioned in the accusation against
him. But an exegetical comparison of the
variants of this saying in the various Gospels shows that his opponents, by their
assertion that Jesus said that he would
destroy the temple *himself,* distorted what
Jesus actually had said, namely: this temple *will* be destroyed (cf. Mark 13:2) and
I will build another which is not built with
human hands[7] (Mark 14:58). The Zealots,
on the other hand, actually had in mind a
new order in a temple built with human
hands.

Already we perceive what is characteristic for Jesus' attitude to all existing institutions: He does not attribute to them
any kind of eternal worth. They belong to
this depraved world, which will pass away.
Since he is convinced that they will perish
with this world, he limits himself on the one
hand to proclaiming their transitoriness,
and on the other hand to cleansing what is

* Scripture quotations are generally from *The Holy
Bible, Revised Standard Version.* New Testament Section,
copyright 1946 by Division of Christian Education of
the National Council of the Churches of Christ in the
United States of America.

possible without a violent destruction of their existence. He does not waste his time in participating in any venture which has as its goal the destruction of institutions by force of arms. For he does not wish to divert hearts from the subject of his sermon: from the kingdom of God, which is not of this world. What he prepares is not the ideal situation of a new priestly organization strived for by the Zealots. The cleansing of the temple is an individual act, a prophetic sign performed by Jesus, and not an element of a Zealot program. It is to guide our attention to the authentic worship in spirit, which will be realized outside the framework of worldly institutions. Jesus wishes to abolish the existing customs connected with the temple cult which stand in flagrant contradiction to the essence of all worship and which already *can* be abolished without the violent destruction of the temple cult. The cleansing of the temple concerns directly only a very limited aspect of Jewish worship.[8] Jesus' attitude is thus restricted.

His attitude, however, is certainly not determined by a tendency to compromise, but rather by an *eschatological radicalism*. Seen from this point of view the revolution for which Jesus worked is more radical than the one which the Zealots sought to realize.[9] For although their future hope presupposes the miraculous assistance of God, it is to be realized in a national-earthly framework.[10] The announcement of the destruction of the temple and the act of cleansing the temple, which was to a limited extent "revolutionary," confirm that Jesus' expectation of the end did not give rise to passivity. Nevertheless, a fundamental difference separated Jesus from Zealotry.

Furthermore, we know that Jesus actually did not condemn the temple worship as such. R. Bultmann, who advocates the same view, rightly points to Matthew 5:23 f., one of the few sayings which he considers to be genuine: "So if you are offering your gift at the altar, and there remember that your brother has something against you, leave your gift there before the altar. . . ."[11] Jesus cleanses the temple cult; he does not seek to eliminate it.

Jesus takes the same attitude to *every* tradition. "Practice," he says, "and observe whatever they [the scribes and Pharisees] tell you, but not what they do" (Matt. 23:

3 f.). The saying of Matthew 23:23 grows out of the same acceptance of the framework of the existing tradition: "One ought to do this (what is *important* in the Law: justice, mercy, faithfulness), but *without neglecting the others* (the many detailed regulations)."[12] As long as the framework of the tradition allows him to proclaim the good news, he holds fast to it. He sets aside, however, with inexorable consistency—in contrast to the Zealots, whose radicalism concerned the letter of the Law—those components of the tradition which hinder him from fulfilling, in a truly radical and uncompromising way, the divine will behind the old Law. As the antitheses of the Sermon on the Mount require, "You have heard ... , but I say to you. ..."

From this radically eschatological obedience to the divine will he arrives then indeed at a position of open opposition to the Pharisees, and his controversy with them was all the sharper since he certainly felt himself much closer to them than to the more religiously indifferent Sadducees. His radical obedience led him to a freedom in relation to the letter of the Law which must be viewed as revolutionary.[13]

We can extend what has been said here

about the temple and the tradition to Jesus' attitude concerning the people of Israel themselves. Jesus respects the special role of Israel: "Go to the lost sheep of the house of Israel." And yet he does not equate Israel with the kingdom of God, to which men "from east and west" will come (Matt. 8:11). Thus it is possible for him, in spite of his acknowledgment of the mission of Israel in God's plan of salvation, which he does not question, to maintain an attitude toward the Samaritans and the Gentiles which must have deeply shocked the Jews, and especially the Zealots, whose hate for the Gentiles was the most extreme.

3 THE SOCIAL QUESTION

Jesus in his proclamation most sharply condemned the *social injustice* of his time. Also here he shared an essential concern of the Zealots. He judged this entire problem in light of the kingdom of God. With the utmost harshness he severely criticized injustice in his sermon: "Woe to you that are rich!" (Luke 6:24).[1] He considered the poor fortunate, for theirs is the kingdom of God. The parable of the

rich man and Lazarus (Luke 16:19 ff.) likewise places the social difference in this
eschatological perspective, and the foolishness of the rich man in the parable of Luke
12:16 ff. is also evident in this light. Does
this mean that Jesus in reality reconciled
himself to the social injustice of the present
world for the duration of the short period of
time before it passes away? Even with respect to the perspective of the imminent
nearness of the end, with which, as we know,
Jesus reckons, this is in no way the case.
Otherwise what purpose should be served
by the directions given to his disciples?

In the yet remaining time before the end
Jesus proclaimed on the one hand that in
light of the coming kingdom the differences
between rich and poor are entirely against
the will of God. This judgment of the present social order is as such revolutionary.
But it is not so in the sense that Jesus called
for the overthrow of this order itself. On
the other hand, in order to prepare his disciples already in the present for the coming
revolution emanating from God, he confronts them with the demand that each
individual is to apply the norms, which are
those of the coming kingdom, already in
his situation. But these norms are not

components of a *revolutionary reform program of the existing institutions.* Soon God will pass sentence on the unjust order. But man *on an individual level* is to be already radically changed by the law of love. He is as such an object of the call of repentance. Bultmann rightly gives special emphasis to this individual character of Jesus' teaching in his *Theology of the New Testament.*[2] As contrary as this priority which Jesus grants to the individual change of heart may be to some modern conceptions, we should not do violence to the texts. This is an undeniable fact. Jesus strives to free us from egoism, hate, deceit, unjust acts. He wishes to change the relationship of man to God and the relationship of man to his neighbor.

"Seek *first* [*prōton*] the kingdom [of God (Matt. 6:33 adds 'and his righteousness')], and all these things will be given ['given into the bargain'] to you."[3] It is significant that in both Matthew and Luke this saying serves as the conclusion to the exhortation not to "be anxious" about the material needs of food, drink, and clothes. These are concerns of the Gentiles. "Your heavenly Father knows that you need these things." Exactly at this point Jesus says:

"Seek first the kingdom [of God]." It is consequently clear how Matthew and Luke (and already the sayings source) understood this saying.

Jesus turns here to the poor and the rich. It would be a distortion of his teaching, however, to view the stressed pre-eminence which he assigns to the seeking of God's kingdom as a means of not disturbing the complacency of the rich. For there can be no doubt: Jesus considers it an injustice that there are poor and rich, and in light of the difficulty which riches present for entrance into the Kingdom of God (Mark 10:23 ff.), he required the rich young ruler to become capable of fulfilling the demand: "Sell what you have, and give to the poor" (Mark 10:21).

Nevertheless, it is not a question here of a social reform program, just as the saying concerning the necessity of hating father and mother, or of not burying the dead, or the saying about eunuchs may not be viewed as elements of a general reform. The universal revolution remains reserved for the establishment of the kingdom of God. But within the yet existing social framework his disciple is already personally to apply in a radical way the norms of the coming kingdom. We could extend Jesus' line of thought and show that the social question would actually be solved already in this age if every individual would become as radically converted as Jesus demands. This is shown perhaps by the story of the rich chief tax collector Zacchaeus (Luke 19:2 ff.) who, without selling all that he had, yet gave half of his goods to the poor.

Although Jesus sharply criticizes social injustice and stresses the necessity of a conversion of the heart so that each person may already in the present overcome the injustice in his area, yet there may be exceptional cases when these directions appear in the background, namely, when it is required by a pressing concern of the kingdom of God. "You always have the poor with you, and whenever you will, you can do good to them" was his response (Mark 14:7) to those in Bethany who blamed the woman who anointed him with costly ointment, which could have been sold and the money given to the poor.

Generally, it must be remembered that Jesus, even according to the presentation of the Gospel of Luke, which is especially concerned about social injustice, bases

every action upon a preceding consideration of his fundamental commitment. The
scene of the story of Mary and Martha
(Luke 10:38 ff.) is characteristic in this
respect even though it takes place in a
limited social framework. The industrious
activism of Martha is indeed praised, yet
seen as insufficient. There is something
higher. "Mary has chosen the good por-
tion." Without overestimating the importance of this story, still it should not be
tacitly passed over. For it confirms what
we have said about Jesus' attitude, namely,
that it is also in this respect more complex
than some think. In the same connection
other passages of the Gospels are to be
recalled which report how Jesus, at the
peak of his success, withdrew from the
crowd.

Our conclusion is analogous to the one
which we made concerning Jesus' attitude
to the temple worship: He severely criticized in his sermons the social injustice in
the existing order. He demanded a radical
individual change of heart, which already
in the present age changes one's relationship to God *and to one's neighbor*. The
whole question is seen in light of the kingdom of God, which has norms that are

entirely different from those of the world and of men.

The first Christians faithfully followed the attitude of their Master. They realized a type of community of goods which, in contrast to that which was imposed upon the members of the Qumran sect, was not obligatory (Acts 4:36 f., 5:1 ff., especially 5:4), but inspired by the Holy Spirit, who worked in the hearts of individuals. Here we see how the priority of the radical individual change demanded by Jesus led to a new order of human relations.

4 THE POLITICAL QUESTION

The questions which we have considered up to this point become even more sharply defined when we proceed to the political question. We have seen that Jesus' crucifixion confronts us from the outset with this problem. Jesus was condemned by Pilate as a political rebel, as a Zealot. And the Zealots themselves, as well as the Romans, could be deceived concerning Jesus' real intentions. We have mentioned that his eschatological expectation led to a critical attitude toward the Roman state and the authorities. Certain sayings and certain actions of Jesus place him actually close to the Zealots, and other acts, such as the cleansing of the temple and the entry into Jerusalem, could only too easily have been interpreted in this sense, if the special character of his Messianic proclamation was not understood. We shall see that the disciples themselves had trouble in freeing themselves from the current Jewish concept of the kingdom of God. The national excitement which Jesus' appearance everywhere evoked must have suggested the notion of a Zealotist revolt. Hence we can understand the hostility of Herod, to whom Jesus' success must have seemed just as suspicious as that of John the Baptist in former times.[1] The fourth Gospel, which has at its disposal good historical traditions for the passion narrative and the immediately preceding events,[2] reports in John 6:15 that the crowd at a certain moment wanted forcefully to take Jesus along and make him king. Sooner or later the national enthusiasm necessarily threatened to take on this form, which urged itself all the more on the crowd since other Zealot

leaders were evidently viewed as kings
of the future kingdom of Israel, which was
identified with the kingdom of God. This is
attested to by sources from the subsequent
period and also recently by the discovery
of two letters of Barkochba in the Dead
Sea region. It is therefore not astonishing
that for Pilate the case of Jesus was in the
same category as the cases of the many
Zealot leaders that he had to judge, indeed
also in the same category as the case of Barabbas, who certainly was a Zealot since he
was taken prisoner, according to Mark 15:7,
"with the rebels" in the "insurrection" and
was designated with an expression applied
to the Zealots.[3]

According to John 11:48 the Sanhedrin
decided to denounce Jesus as a political
rebel to the Romans for fear that they
would be held responsible in case the
popular movement supporting Jesus should
take on disturbing proportions. I cannot
repeat here the entire argumentation for
the thesis that Pilate did not simply ratify
a judgment given by the Jews, but rather
himself had to judge Jesus. For this I
would refer the reader to my work, *The
State in the New Testament*.[4] Actually it
was from the beginning the *Roman* cohort

who arrested Jesus in Gethsemane. He was therefore the prisoner of the Romans. The preliminary hearing before the high priest was more of a moral interrogation which Pilate had wished in order to be certain that he would not offend the Jewish authorities. The actual trial was the trial before Pilate, and hence a political trial. The *moral* responsibility therefore lay completely on the side of the high priest,[5] the *legal* on the other hand entirely on the side of the Romans.

Thus Jesus suffered the *Roman* death penalty, crucifixion, and the inscription, the "titulus," above the cross named as his crime the Zealotist attempt of having strived for kingly rule in Israel, a country still administered by the Romans.

These facts, which are today considered as historically reliable, are readily mentioned by those who wish to make Jesus into a Zealotist revolutionary. Is it justifiable, however, to conclude that Jesus really *was* a Zealot from the correct assertion that he was denounced and crucified as a Zealot? Certainly this is a premature conclusion. A careful investigation of Jesus' attitude to the political question of his day proves, on the contrary, that his con-

demnation was the result of a judicial
error. The essence of his eschatological
attitude was not understood by the Gentiles, and indeed could not have been understood by them.[6]

We need, therefore, to investigate his
conception of Messianism. We have seen
that the Gospels unanimously report that
Jesus withdrew from mass movements, as
for example just at the moment when the
people wanted to crown him king (John
6:15). To be sure, he seems to have not
directly attacked the Zealots and the
Sicarii whereas he did directly attack the
Pharisees.[7] Nevertheless, the Zealots themselves must have known that Jesus, in spite
of his sympathy for certain aspects of their
movement, was never a member of their
party and never worked together with
them.

It can be asked whether Jesus had the
Zealots in mind in his somewhat obscure
saying concerning the "men of violence
who try to bring about the kingdom of God
and take possession of it by force" (Matt.
11:12).[8] It is not certain whether this saying is to be considered a reproach or a
word of praise. The Greek expression,
which we translate with "force," seems

rather to suggest the idea of a reproach.
Perhaps the saying is intentionally used
ambiguously. In this case it would corre-
spond to the double feeling which Jesus had
toward the Zealots. The Johannine chapter
about the "good shepherd" (John 10)
appears to me to allude to certain Zealot
leaders who deliver their followers over
to the Romans to be slaughtered. This
seems to me to be by far the most probable,
if not entirely certain, explanation of this
passage about the false shepherds (v. 8):
"All who came before me are thieves and
robbers."[9] The false shepherd ("hire-
ling"), says Jesus, does not spare the life
of the sheep whereas the true shepherd
"lays down his life for his sheep." This
may indeed be based upon an authentic saying of Jesus. Even if the martyrdom of certain Zealot leaders must be acknowledged,
the Gospel of John clearly distinguishes the
sacrifice of Jesus from theirs: "No one
takes [my life] from me, but I lay it down
of my own accord" (v. 18).

This leads us to the real core of our
problem. Firstly, did Jesus ascribe to himself a *direct* role not only in the announcement but also in the actual bringing about
of the kingdom of God? And secondly: if

we reply affirmatively to the first question, how did he *perceive* this role? The Bultmann school gives a negative answer to the first question. Accordingly, Jesus was conscious only of *announcing the* kingdom of God in the manner of the Old Testament prophets. Over against this assertion the following objection seems to me to present itself: The judicial error of the Romans would not have been possible, and the priestly Jewish authorities would not have been able to denounce Jesus to the Romans as a Zealot leader who strived for kingly rule in Israel, if a claim of Jesus, in whatever way it was expressed, had not actually been made, which could have by distortion been interpreted in the sense of the political Messiah expected by the majority of Jews. That the Roman accusation concerned a claim of Jesus follows from the inscription above the cross,[10] the "titulus" which according to Roman custom[11] specified the crime for which he was condemned. (An analogous sign was most likely placed above the crosses of the two thieves.) Actually, this fact as such, apart from the exceptional character which the Gospel of John incorrectly attributes to it,[12] can hardly be denied.[13]

In order to answer the second question, concerning the true character of what is called Jesus' "Messianic consciousness," it must be remembered that at the time of Jesus there were in Judaism two very different concepts of the Messiah. According to the one, which was more or less official and shared by the majority of people, the Messiah was a victorious warrior, who as king on earth will establish a powerful kingdom of Israel through which God would then rule over the world. According to the other, advocated by certain small groups, the kingdom of God will be realized in a cosmic framework beyond earthly circumstances by the "Son of Man" of the book of Daniel and apocryphal apocalypses, who will come "on the clouds of heaven." I cannot develop here anew my thesis that Jesus did not regard himself as a political Messiah, but rather as the Son of Man, and that he was simultaneously conscious of fulfilling in his person the mission of the "Suffering Servant" of whom Deutero-Isaiah speaks.[14] Jesus' explanations regarding the special task entrusted to him by God concern the Son of Man and the Servant of God.

Whether or not one shares this interpretation, it is in any case certain that Jesus viewed the political conception of Messiah always as a temptation, and indeed as *his special temptation*. For this reason Matthew and Luke place the temptation narrative, which is designed to portray this fact, at the beginning of his public ministry. The Devil is the one who showed Jesus the kingdoms of the world: "All these I will give to you." He proposes to him the Zealot ideal. But Jesus replies: "Begone, Satan!" (Matt. 4:10). One is tempted only by those things which are close to him. In light of the burning expectation of the Zealots, which was shared by several disciples of Jesus, and in light of his great success with the crowd which offered him kingly rule, the idea must have come to his mind that perhaps he was to realize already on earth the kingdom of God. Whatever the historical core of the temptation narrative may be, certainly behind it stands the fact which can be followed throughout the Gospels, namely, that Jesus viewed the Zealotist political concept of Messiah as a satanic temptation. "Begone, Satan!"

Jesus sees exactly the same temptation, the same Devil at work in the conversation on the way to Caesarea Philippi (Mark

8:27-33). At this moment the Devil makes
use of the apostle Peter, who wishes to prevent Jesus from fulfilling his role as the
Suffering Servant of God: "This shall
never happen to you!", whereupon Jesus
responds to Peter with a rebuke entirely
analogous to that in the temptation narrative: "Get behind me, Satan!" That proves
that Peter was not able to free himself from
the official Jewish, political, and hence satanic conception when he declared: "You
are the Messiah." He had thought of the
political Messiah, who was not meant to
suffer.[15]

The third temptation, which Luke expressly sets in relation to the first, takes
place in Gethsemane. This is the "opportune time" for which the Devil according
to Luke 4:13 waited: the final temptation.
Jesus is tempted to shrink back from death.
According to Luke (22:49) certain of his
disciples are armed.[16] The Roman cohort
approaches. Would it not be possible to
kindle a popular revolt? Has the moment
not come when the Zealot ideal, the holy
war, is to become a reality? And would not
God assist him with "more than twelve
legions" (Matt. 26:53)? Jesus resists this
decisive temptation. "Put your sword back

into its place'' (Matt. 26:52). He is arrested by the Romans and his disciples flee.

In the Jewish conception of the Messianic king faith and politics are closely connected. Therein lies exactly the temptation. For this reason Jesus always observes the greatest restraint toward the title of Messiah when it is conferred on him. He knows that this title gives rise to misunderstandings, and the events have only all too well confirmed this. Without totally refusing the title—if it had been emptied of its political connotations, he could indeed have accepted it—he prefers to keep away from it. For this reason he commands silence every time he is called Messiah. This explanation, which is fully anchored in the historical situation, seems to me to make the well-known theory of W. Wrede[17] superfluous. According to this theory, which has been made a dogma by some exegetes, Jesus' command of silence was a later invention of Mark in order to explain the fact that Jesus' Messiahship, unrecognized during his lifetime, was first proclaimed after Easter. But on the way to Caesarea Philippi Jesus neither confirms nor rejects Peter's statement: ''You are the Messiah.'' He knows that Peter still holds to the satanic conception, and therefore proceeds with an explanation not concerning the Messiah, but concerning the Son of Man and the Suffering Servant. At various times I have pointed out that according to Matthew 26:64 Jesus' answer to the question of the high priest: "Are you the Messiah?", when traced back to the Aramaic, does not simply mean "Yes," but: "You have said so" (not I). This answer, if not directly negative, is in any case evasive,[18] as is confirmed by the parallel, entirely differently phrased Lucan text (Luke 22:67). According to John 18:36 Jesus replies to the political question of Pilate (the only one which interested him), "Are you the King of the Jews?" with the decisive answer, which I could have used as motto for this presentation: *"My kingdom is not of this world."*

But did Jesus not after all give in to the temptation at the moment of his *entry into Jerusalem?* Was this not, as is often said, the decisive act through which Jesus wished to set up the Messianic kingdom on a national level? Certainly this event, if it was actually observed by Jesus' opponents, would have been exploited by them in order to convince the Romans of the dangerous

character of this preacher. Actually the
Gospel accounts of this event have given
rise to many exegetical discussions. According to one viewpoint the event which lies
behind these accounts definitely did not
take place at the time of Jesus' entry into
Jerusalem, and certainly does not deserve
the significance attributed to it by the
Evangelists. Thus a few of Jesus' followers, at a certain time and at a place unknown to us, paid homage to him although
he never asked for this, and the entire
event remained more or less unnoticed.[19]
However this may be, if Jesus pursued a
special intention (which is not certain),
then it must be observed that he chose precisely the donkey (in accordance with Zech.
9:9) and not the horse in the manner of a
warlike Messiah, thereby demonstrating in
this case the peaceful character of his entry.

We are now acquainted, therefore, with
the special nature of Jesus' Messianism.
His expectation of the kingdom of God had
to lead him to a critical attitude toward
the Roman empire. Jesus could have viewed
the occupation of Palestine by the Romans
only as a usurpation by violent men, for
their totalitarian claim, according to which
Caesar demanded what belongs to God,

must have been known to him. He concedes
no more divine right to the emperor than
to Herod, the "fox" who wanted to kill
him.

All this must have made Jesus likable to
the Zealots and explains why Zealots felt
attracted to him and even became his disciples. And yet he did not join them, for
their goal and their methods were not his.
Jesus preached insurrection neither against
Herod, who persecuted him, nor against the
emperor. He was as far removed from a
revolt against the state as from an uncon-
ditional inner acceptance of it. Both of
these positions would have been incompati-
ble with his message of the good news of
the kingdom of God. Among the Twelve
was one or more former Zealots. No false
conclusion, however, as is often the case,
should be drawn from this. For what is
especially worthy of attention, as has been
noted, is that he accepted into the Twelve
also a (indeed former) tax collector, i.e., a
representative of those who collaborated
with the occupation force and therefore
were deeply hated by the Jews and especially by the Zealots. Jesus sought even the
company of these representatives of the
existing political order.

Also the *love of one's enemy*, which he required in the name of the kingdom of God, places him beyond the warring political forces. He excludes every use of force as it was preached by the Zealots.

Nothing illustrates more clearly his double attitude toward the state—on the one hand a critical attribute, on the other hand an acceptance of its existence until its coming disappearance—than the answer given by Jesus to the question of the Herodians and the Pharisees: "Is it allowed to pay taxes to Caesar, or not?" (Matt. 22:17). His opponents thus want to expose him. If he answers "Yes," he will be considered a traitor with respect to the God of Israel. If he answers "No," then he confesses that he is a rebel. Again Jesus says neither Yes nor No. His answer, with respect to the unacceptable alternatives presented him, is intentionally ambiguous: "Give to Ceasar the things that are Caesar's, and to God the things that are God's" (Matt. 22:21). To the Zealots, who answered the question whether one should pay taxes with a categorical "No" and for whom this question was a test of one's faithfulness to Israel, Jesus' answer must have seemed a deplorable compromise. Hence by all means they had to condemn Jesus although, as we have seen, he never directly condemned the Zealots. Even if they had had no other reason, this answer must have been for them enough.

In reality it was neither diplomatic considerations nor a tendency to compromise, but rather Jesus' faithfulness to the message of the kingdom of God which *had to* lead him to give exactly the answer we know: Give to the state what it needs for its existence (for it will be destroyed by God, not by you), "Give [back] to Caesar the things that are Caesar's. . . ." But that includes at the same time: Give him no more than those things (thus in case he demands more, refuse it). ". . . and to God the things that are God's." This part of the sentence should not be taken to infer that God and Caesar are on the same level. For in this case Jesus would have clearly placed himself on the side of the Herodians, and such an attitude would have been entirely acceptable to representatives of the existing political order. In reality there is irony, a literary device indeed often used by Jesus, contained in this saying.[20] What should be given to Caesar? Money. We recall what Jesus says in other places about

God and mammon. One gives money (back) to Caesar, for it belongs to him. But one gives to God what belongs to *him*: our entire person. Because this answer lies beyond a simple Yes or No, his opponents were able to distort it, as they distorted what he said concerning his divine vocation. According to Luke 23:2 the Jews led Jesus to Pilate with the accusation: "We found this man perverting our nation, and forbidding us to give tribute to Caesar."

Jesus' position regarding the Zealot question seems to me on the whole so clear that it may be allowed to explain from the same perspective the puzzling saying about the *sword* which the disciples, according to Luke 22:36, are to procure: "Let him who has no sword sell his mantle and buy one."[21] It is important that this saying not be isolated from the other sayings of Jesus about the sword. When he says in Matthew 10:34 that he has not come to bring peace, but the sword, Jesus by no means *recommends* a holy war, but rather confirms that the decision to which his sermon calls men will cause dissension, and at the same time prepares his disciples for the persecution.[22] The previously cited command to buy a sword also refers to the time of persecution. Again here it would be easy to avoid the difficulty of the explanation by denying the authenticity of the saying, and viewing it therefore as a "community-formation."[23]

Without wishing absolutely to exclude this possibility of its being a "community-formation," I find the arguments listed for this thesis inadequate. If the saying, as is my opinion, is authentic, it warns the disciples against believing that they will have the gospel to preach in a peaceful atmosphere. On the contrary, they will be exposed to attacks (even armed) when they preach the good news. This is no summons to a holy war. There may be times when the disciple individually is to defend himself if he is attacked while carrying out his mission, but he is not to take part in military ventures.[24] We find the actual intention of the saying or rather narrative, however, expressed only at the end. In reply to Jesus' command the disciples say: "Here are two swords," and Jesus answers: "It is enough." This does not mean that the two swords are sufficient. On the basis of the preceding conclusions I would suggest once again that this was Jesus' way of breaking off the dialogue. As soon as he

realizes that the disciples, by their immediate display of two swords, understand his
recommendation to buy a sword in the
sense of Zealotism, he restrains them: It is
enough! Likewise he commanded silence
when the ambiguous title of Messiah was
conferred on him. According to the same
22nd chapter of the Gospel of Luke the disciples in Gethsemane put the Zealot question to Jesus: "Shall we strike with the
sword?" (v. 49). Then as one actually drew
his sword, Jesus said again (v. 51): "No
more of this!" There is a limit set to resistance. It is at the point where resistance is
transformed into violent revolt.

We can conclude with a final saying
handed down to us by Luke (23:28 ff.),
which is too often neglected in the debate
over our problem. In it we also find con-
firmation for the view presented here. On
the way to Golgotha Jesus says to the
weeping women: "Daughters of Jerusalem,
do not weep for me, but weep for yourselves
and for your children. . . . For *if they do
this to the green wood, what shall be done
to the dry?*" Evidently the subject "they"
in the preceding sentence refers to the
Romans, who are about to put Jesus to
death. Jesus designates himself as the

49

"green wood" to whom they will do this. Hence there is only one possible explanation. Jesus means: if the Romans put him to death as a Zealot, who is no Zealot and who has always warned against essential characteristics of the Zealots—if they put him to death, who therefore is "green wood," what will they one day do with the true Zealots ("dry wood")? It is a final prediction. In the manner of the Old Testament prophets Jesus prophesies what will be fulfilled forty years later: the victory of the Romans over the Jewish insurrectionists, who by then will have proceeded to open warfare. We find confirmed here that Jesus was condemned as a Zealot, but at the same time that he *was no Zealot*, although he took an interest in this parallel and yet so different movement during his entire ministry.

Certainly he bitterly disappointed the Zealots, and this disappointment may have played a part in Judas' betrayal of him. The early Christians, however, followed in the footprints of their Master. For at the time when the Jewish War broke out they did not join together with the Zealots, but fled to the other side of the Jordan.[25]

5 CONCLUDING REMARKS

J esus' attitude to the
three problems discussed above demon-
strates a remarkable uniformity. It is gov-
erned by an eschatological radicalism. This
leads on the one side to an unreserved criticism of the existing order, but on the other
side also to a rejection of resistance movements, since these divert one's attention
from the kingdom of God with their setting
of goals, and violate by their use of vio-

lence the command to absolute justice and absolute love.

I have endeavored to remain firmly rooted in Biblical exegesis. From the results others may now attempt to make the applications for our day. I would like in conclusion to show only the problems which present themselves in practice, and at least try to indicate the direction in which solutions can perhaps be found.

First of all I would point to the exceptional difficulty of the problem. For the reality that Jesus' attitude *cannot be simply* transferred into our time proceeds from the fact that we no longer reckon with an imminent end of the world. A type of "adaptation" to the present is therefore necessary. But exactly here the problems begin. For all adaptation (or as one likes to say today in connection with the solution of the Second Vatican Council, "*aggiornamento*") is indeed easy when one limits himself to one-sidedly orienting his interpretation of the Biblical directives and commands so that contemporary man may be able to understand and affirm them in connection with his own problems. But the principal task, and thus the principal difficulty, consists in the endeavor to translate the message of Jesus into our time without either surrendering or weakening its fundamental character. For that would no longer mean adaptation, but rather betrayal.

Yet here a preliminary question first presents itself: Is such a translation not ultimately impossible? Is it not asking too much of Jesus when we wish to standardize our attitude to the existing orders or to revolution on the basis of his teaching and life? We have seen that in light of his expectation of the end Jesus cannot even be placed in one of the groups of his time. How then is this to be possible with respect to present-day groups? Is the slogan referring to a religion which withdraws from the world as an "opiate of the masses" not to an increased extent applicable to Jesus' teaching? Here, however, the further question is to be placed whether Jesus' expectation of the coming kingdom really involves withdrawing from the world, whether the world as a place of action affirmed by Jesus must not be distinguished from the world as the norm of action denied by him, and whether his hope does not above all provide for him the impulse to strive for justice in a world destined to perish, as long it still endures, and indeed within *all* existing groups. From this point a translation into the circumstances of our time is shown, in spite of all difficulties, to be in principle possible.

Such a translation is after all hardly questioned by our modern world with its intense stress on "secularization" and "technicalization." Without wishing to underestimate these two phenomena, it seems to me that our age, because of a certain proud exultation which can also be observed repeatedly in past ages, exaggerates the degree of change of the situation *insofar as it is of importance for the proclamation of the gospel.* We should not forget that already in the first century the immediate reaction of the Graeco-Roman world to the sermon of the apostle Paul was the laughter of the Athenians on the Areopagus. Certainly Paul adapted himself—"to the Jews a Jew, to the Greeks a Greek"—but he did not, in order to prevent this laughter, change the strange nature, even for the world at this time, of the gospel, the "foolishness of God."

I do not wish, however, in this way to diminish the established difficulty of the problem. On the contrary, I consider a translation at *one* important point as plainly impossible. I am referring to the already mentioned imminent expectation of Jesus. It is certain that for centuries Jesus did not reckon with the continuation of the world. Here a difference actually exists between him and us which is much more important than what is said of the secularization and technicalization of our world. This difference, which has only recently been recognized, has consequences for *one* aspect of our special problem, namely, for the fact that Jesus was concerned *only* with the conversion of the individual and was not interested in a reform of the social structures. But as soon as centuries are reckoned with, it must necessarily be acknowledged that more just social structures also promote the individual change of character required by Jesus. A reciprocal action is therefore required between the conversion of the individual and the reform of the structures, even though the former must remain the principal factor in the life of the Christian.

Jesus' imminent expectation and his resulting neglect of the social structures are important aspects for a suitable understanding of the problem of application to our time. They do not, however, justify the

renunciation of every "application" in
general. For Jesus' hope does not stand
or fall with the specific form of the imminent expectation, and Jesus' requirement
concerning the *priority* of seeking the kingdom of God before all social endeavors does
not fall away as superfluous, even when we
today consider a working together of individual conversion and reform of the struc-
ures as essential. The eschatological basis
of Jesus' behavior retains its validity even
when we know that the world continues for
centuries. Should not our reform-minded
age exactly in the interest of reforms take
entirely seriously Jesus' exhortation to a
conversion of the heart, which also includes
nonviolence? Will not that working together
be again excluded, or at least diminished, if
this necessity is not acknowledged?

I have briefly pointed out in the chapter
about the social question that the early
Christians, in accordance with the teachings of Jesus, practiced a nonobligatory,
i.e., based upon the voluntary decision of
the individual, type of community of goods.
On the basis of this practice, even though it
was after all realized only in the earliest
period of early Christianity and did not yet
signify the creation of an actual social

structure, it is at least at the beginning
clear how the conversion of the individual
can inspire social reforms and how these
can be standardized on the basis of Jesus'
teaching even though they lie outside the
range of his perspective.

Christians, who today share responsibility for reforms, should freely and com-
petently make use of the technical means
which the modern world offers them, but
they should not wish to declare that along
with their technical proficiency they also
take their ultimate norms from the world
instead of from the gospel.

The eschatological radicalism of Jesus,
as we have seen, underlies his absolute
obedience to the will of God and the resulting condemnation of legalism, hypoc-
risy, and injustice. The Zealots also proceed from an eschatological radicalism; but
Jesus is much more radical not only with
respect to his concept of the kingdom of
God, but also with respect to his application
of norms. His goal and norms are "not of
this world," as is the case for the Zealots.
For this reason he directs his criticism not
only against the defenders of the existing
order, but also against the Zealots. That
does not infer that it is Jesus' intention

that we should in general eliminate our ethical judgment by indiscriminately including all in the same criticism. I have vigorously stressed that Jesus found himself in a certain sense close to the Zealots— as also to the Pharisees.[1] There was for him a Zealotist temptation. But exactly for that reason he warned those to whom he found himself close of the terrible consequences of their fundamental position, which made all their efforts so questionable and ultimately caused them to be transformed from nonconformists into conformists. Their resistance became indeed finally so popular in Palestine that it required courage to criticize them for not taking their norms from the kingdom which is not of this world.

If we are here carefully to show how Jesus' attitude can be applied today, then we shall say that there are limits set to the cooperation of the Christian with "worldly," non-Christian groups which he sees as representing an ideal close to the gospel. He is freely to seek contact with such groups and be glad that they are perhaps closer to the kingdom of God than others who call themselves Christian, and he is to work together with them where he shares their goals and methods. But he will render them a service only if he does not simply repeat mechanically what they say, but also says something different to them from a standpoint which after all differs from theirs. Above all he will dare to give a decisive "No" where goals are pursued and methods are employed which are contrary to the gospel. Does the church today always resist the temptation implied here?

It is gratifying that contemporary Christians feel an obligation to the world as seldom before. But they should endeavor all the more not to be ashamed of the gospel (Rom. 1:16) exactly at the point where it is foolishness for the world (I Cor. 1:18 ff.), and this pertains indeed to both conformists and nonconformists. The apostle Paul applied with remarkable faithfulness to Christians what the preceding presentation proposes as the teaching and attitude of Jesus when he writes to the Corinthians (I Cor. 7:31) that they are "to use the things of this world as though they did not use them," and to the Romans (Rom. 12:2): "Do not be conformed to this world, but be transformed by the *renewal of your mind.*" These exhortations retain their value alongside the absolute necessity of working *in* the world and *for* the world, and alongside the necessity of making oneself understood by it. The author of the Letter to Diognetus, who as hardly anyone else grasped the double demand of the New Testament concerning the position of Jesus' disciples to the world, describes the Christians of the second half of the second century (V—VI) as people who in no way isolate themselves from others and participate in all their activities: "they live in the world, but are not of the world" (Diog. VI. 3).

NOTES

1 THE PROBLEM

1. Translated from the German, and published 1910.

2. M. Hengel, *Die Zeloten. Untersuchungen zur jüdischen Freiheitsbewegung in der Zeit von Herodes I. bis 70 n. Chr.*, 1961. See also W. R. Farmer, *Maccabees, Zealots and Josephus*, 1956.

3. G. Baumbach, "Zeloten und Sikarier," *Theologische Literaturzeitung*, 1965, pp. 727 ff. Further "Die Zelotenihre geschichtliche und religionspolitische Bedeutung," *Bibel und Liturgie*, vol. 41, 1968, pp. 2 ff. In the latter he also treats briefly the problem, "Jesus und die Zeloten." Although he strongly differs in some particulars, he comes to conclusions similar to those of my 1956 publication, *The State in the New Testament*, and of my 1962 lecture, "Die Bedeutung der Zelotenbewegung im Neuen Testament," now in *Oscar Cullmann, Vorträge und Aufsätze 1925-1962*, 1966, pp. 292 ff. See especially also in the same volume, pp. 214 ff., "Der zwölfte Apostel."

4. Y. Yadin, *Masada: Herod's Fortress and the Zealots' Last Stand*, 1966. W. Eck, "Die Eroberung von Masada und eine neue Inschrift des L. Flavius Silva Nonius Bassus," *Zeitschrift für die neutestamentliche Wissenschaft und die Kunde der älteren Kirche*, 1969, pp. 282 ff. Eck accepts with M. Hengel the year A.D. 74 rather than A.D. 73.—The present State of Israel has made a national holy place of the Masada fortress which can be seen by visitors.

5. See pp. 33 f. below.

6. See pp. 31 f. and 33 f. below.

7. *Von dem Zwecke Jesu und seiner Jünger,* published by G. E. Lessing in 1778 as vol. 7 of his *Fragmente eines Ungenannten.*

8. *Der Ursprung des Christentums,* 1908. Kantsky, however, who was a Socialist, was primarily interested in this thesis from a political standpoint.

9. *Iesous basileus ou basileusas,* 2 vols., 1929-30.

10. *Jesus and the Zealots,* 1967. Brandon indeed does not designate Jesus as a Zealot, but understands his life and teaching entirely in connection with Zealotism. Although the author does not conceal his sympathy for the Zealots and for revolutions, his argumentation is carefully supported.—Joel Carmichael (*The Death of Jesus,* 1962) is perhaps not personally responsible for the sensation which has been made out of his not new principal thesis concerning the condemnation of Jesus by the Romans and Jesus' connection with the Zealots. He endeavors to show the development from the actual history to its "distortion" by an exegetical comparison of the Gospels. However, since he enters into no discussion with the past or present research, although he is, as he admits, extensively indebted to it, his entire construction lacks a scholarly self-criticism.

11. This is how he is named in Luke's lists of the disciples (Luke 6:15 and Acts 1:13). Mark (3:19) and Matthew (10:4) call him "kananaios," which may not be translated "Canaanite," since it is simply the Greek transcription of the Aramaic translation of Zealot. (Cf. Hebrew *qna,* zeal.) The inconclusive assertion of Brandon, *op. cit.,* that Mark wanted to conceal with this transcription the fact that Simon was a Zealot,

is connected with the thesis that Brandon defends throughout his book, viz., that Mark wanted to de-politicize the gospel.

12. The proponents of the thesis that Jesus was a Zealot mostly affirm, however without being able to give a valid reason, that Simon remained a Zealot after becoming a disciple of Jesus. We will establish that, according to the attitude of Jesus himself, this supposition is very improbable.

13. In *Peter: Disciple, Apostle, Martyr*, 1962 (2nd ed.), pp. 23 f., and in *The State in the New Testament* I have pointed out that the explanation Barjona=son of John (John 1:42) is not at all certain, and that according to an old Hebrew lexicon cited by G. Dalman in his *Aramäisch-neuhebräisches Wörter-buch*, 1922 (2nd ed.), p. 65a, *barjona* is a word bor-rowed from Accadian and means "terrorist." (See also R. Eisler, *op. cit.*, p. 67.) Cf. M. Hengel, *op. cit.*, pp. 55 ff., who, without entirely excluding this hypothesis, indeed questions the use of the word "Barjona" in the sense of rebel in Matt. 16:17.

14. Convincing evidence is furnished, I believe, in "Der zwölfte Apostel," *op. cit.* I have shown that the mentioning of two Judases in the lists of the Twelve which Luke offers (Luke 6:16 and Acts 1:13) is ex-plained by a duplication which originated from the various designations for one and the same Judas. This is attested to by the textual variants for both Judases, which refer to his (previous) belonging to the Zealots.

15. See p. 34 below.

16. I was not able to mention his freedom from the Law, which certainly is to be taken simultaneously into account and which in a certain sense amounts to a revolutionary attitude, as a similarity to the Zealots

in the previous paragraph, because their radicalism, in contrast, was largely an obedience to the Law, and directly in the sense of an intensified obedience to the letter of the Law rather than in the sense of the antitheses of the Sermon on the Mount: "but I say unto you. . . ."

17. The thesis that Jesus was in agreement with the Zealots is usually based on a fundamental assertion which especially S. G. F. Brandon, *op. cit.*, pp. 245 ff., following other authors has developed: it was the Gospels which first made a pacifist out of the warlike Jesus. Above all Mark was responsible for the "depoliticizing" (see n. 11 above). G. Baumbach, *Die Zeloten*, pp. 19 ff., endeavors, by the use of formcritical considerations, to deny this pacifistic tendency of the Evangelists.

18. Indeed the Zealots also had an intensive future hope; but the kingdom which they expected was "of this world," even though it involved a miraculous intervention of God.

2 THE QUESTION OF WORSHIP

1. *Jésus,* 1950 (2nd ed.), pp. 327 f.

2. *Das Evangelium des Markus*, 1937, p. 237.

3. *Leben Jesu*, 1840, (4th ed.), pp. 731 ff. (quoted by G. Baumbach, *Die Zeloten*, p. 21, n. 129).

4. R. Bultmann, *The History of the Synoptic Tradition*, 1963, appears to accept the historicity. Also H. Braun, *Jesus, der Mann aus Nazareth und seine Zeit*, 1969, p. 78, does not deny it.

5. Et. Trocmé, "L'expulsion des marchands du Temple," *New Testament Studies*, vol. 15, 1968, pp. 1 ff., uses the expression, "Zealotist act" (geste zélote,

p. 19) and points out that the influence of the tradition of Phinehas, the "Zealot for the Law," was very strong in Judaism of the first century A.D. He does not, however, view Jesus as a member of the Zealots.

6. *Ibid.*, pp. 17 f., stresses also that the importance of the event should not be overestimated.

7. The "false witness" (Mark 14:57 f.) may have consisted in the false witnesses using the first person in the first part of the saying. The Johannine form of the beginning of this saying (John 2:19), "Destroy this temple" (i.e., if this temple is destroyed), may be the closest to the original.

8. See also Et. Trocmé, *op. cit.*, pp. 17 ff.

9. Also more radical than the one for which the Essenes strived. See H. Braun, *Spätjüdisch-häretischer und frühchristlicher Radikalismus: Jesus von Nazareth und die essenische Qumransekte*, 2 vols., 1966.

10. According to Hengel, *Die Zeloten. Untersuchungen zur jüdischen Freiheitsbewegung in der Zeit von Herodes I. bis 70 n. Chr.*, 1961, p. 317, their hope is in this sense transcendent and national at the same time.

11. *Theology of the New Testament* I, 1951, p. 17.

12. *Ibid.*, pp. 15 f. Bultmann points indeed to the fact that this saying is missing in the manuscript D rendition of Luke 11:42, but he reckons, however, with the possibility of its authenticity, and then sees in it evidence that "a reform-oriented polemic against the Law was far from the intention" of Jesus.

13. K. Niederwimmer, in his psychologically-oriented presentation of Jesus (*Jesus*, 1968), calls Jesus in this sense a "rebel" (p. 54).

3 THE SOCIAL QUESTION

1. Even if the "cries of woe" of Luke 6:24 ff. are not authentic (they are missing in Matthew), and the verses here mentioned are attributed to the Lucan ideal of poverty, they do not contradict the overall attitude of Jesus. See also Matt. 6:24 and Luke 16:13.

2. Pp. 9 ff., especially p. 19: Jesus' proclamation of the will of God is "not an ethic of world reform," but "an ethic which makes the individual immediately responsible to God."

3. This saying also occurs in Luke (12:31). The word "first" is not in his text, but the idea is here and hence must also have been present in the sayings source used by Matthew and Luke.

4 THE POLITICAL QUESTION

1. Herod's relation to Jesus has been especially well worked out by M. Goguel, *Jésus,* 1950 (2nd ed.), pp. 281 ff.

2. See *ibid.,* and C. H. Dodd, *Historical Tradition in the Fourth Gospel,* pp. 21 ff.

3. *lāstās.* See K. H. Rengstorf, *Theologisches Wörter-buch,* vol. 4, article on *lāstās,* p. 267. The historicity of the Barabbas scene is more and more generally accepted; see, e.g., G. Bornkamm, *Jesus of Nazareth,* 1956, p. 164.

4. *The State in the New Testament,* 1956, 1967 (2nd ed.). My explanations have been largely taken over and carried further by P. Winter, "Marginal Notes on

the Trial of Jesus," *Zeitschrift für Neutestamentliche Wissenschaft*, 1959, pp. 14 ff. and pp. 221 ff., and *On the Trial of Jesus*, 1961. Long before my work H. Lietzmann published his basic essay, "Der Prozess Jesu" (*Sitzungsberichte der Berliner Akademie der Wissenschaften, philosophisch-historische Klasse*, 1931, pp. 313 ff.), which gave rise to a fertile discussion in *Zeitschrift für Neutestamentliche Wissenschaft*, 1931-34. Contrast J. Blinzler, *Der Prozess Jesu*, 1951, 1960 (3rd ed.), who in the sense of Mark and Matthew estimates the role of the Sanhedrin much higher.

5. *Not* on the side of the Jewish people as a whole.

6. Likewise the modern misunderstandings concerning Jesus' relation to the Zealots result from an undifferentiated consideration of Jesus' eschatology.

7. This fact is argued persuasively by S. G. F. Brandon, *Jesus and the Zealots*, 1967, p. 201.—Only after the completion of the present work did I discover in the *Evangelische Kommentare*, no. 12, 1969, pp. 694 ff., the just published six theses of M. Hengel concerning the theme, "War Jesus Revolutionär?", which point in the same direction as the viewpoint represented here. He answers the question concerning the absence of an anti-Zealotist polemic in Jesus' sayings by considering Jesus' opposition to the Pharisees to include also the Zealots, who according to Josephus shared the Pharisees' teachings.

8. This explanation is all the more forceful since the rabbis later reproached the Zealots for attempting to bring about the end by force.

9. The explanation seems all the more convincing since the Greek word (*lāstās*), which we have translated with "robbers," was, as we have seen (see p. 33

above), one of the designations for the Zealots. See K. H. Rengstorf, *op. cit.*, pp. 264 ff.—A. Schlatter's explanation (*Der Evangelist Johannes*, 1930) of this passage, according to which the prophets are meant here, does not seem to me possible.—The interpretation which I am suggesting here is also presented by T. de la Potterie in his "Le bon berger" in *Populus Dei. Studi in Onori del Card. Ottaviani*, 1969, pp. 939 ff.

10. This argument seems fundamental to me for the entire discussion over the role which Jesus ascribed to himself.

11. See Sueton, *Caligula* 32, *Domitian* 10; Dio Cassius 54.8. The fact is also confirmed by Eusebius' report about the martyrs of Lyon, *Historica Ecclesiastica* V.1.44: the martyrs were required to wear signs stating the reason for their condemnation.

12. See John 19:19 ff., which relates the protest of the high priests and Pilate's answer.

13. It is not evident why H. Braun, *Jesus*, p. 50, in following R. Bultmann (*Geschichte der synoptischen Tradition*, p. 293), is of the opinion that he has to deny the historicity affirmed by the majority of exegetes (H. Lietzmann, *op. cit.*, p. 320; M. Dibelius, "Das historische Problem der Leidensgeschichte," *Zeitschrift für die neutestamentliche Wissenschaft* 30, 1931, p. 200; E. Dinkler, "Petrusbekenntnis und Satanswort. Das Problem der Messianität Jesu," in *Zeit und Geschichte, Dankesgabe an R. Bultmann zum 80. Geburtstag*, 1964, p. 148; and many others.) Braun's argumentation here seems to me contradictory. For in the following sentence he acknowledges that Jesus appeared to the Romans to be a troublemaker and that Jewish opponents may have denounced him to the Romans as politically suspicious. In this case

the non-Jewish form of the inscription is not an argument against the historicity, as Braun contends, but rather it confirms it.

14. Cf. *The Christology of the New Testament*, 1963 (2nd ed.).

15. I have shown in *Peter: Disciple, Apostle, Martyr*, 1962 (2nd ed.), that the part of the narrative of Matt. 16:13-25 which Matthew and Mark offer in common (i.e., without the word of praise given by Jesus to Peter) should not carry the title "Peter's Confession," but rather "Rejection of the Satanic Messiah Conception." In reality Matthew conbined this narrative of the rejection with the entirely different narrative involving a confession of Peter not concerning the Messiah, but concerning the Son of God and followed by Jesus' praise of Peter. With regard to the history-of-tradition relationships and the redactional connections see especially my article, "L'apôtre Pierre, instrument du diable et instrument de Dieu," *New Testament Essays for T. W. Manson*, 1959, p. 14, now in German in *Oscar Cullmann. Vorträge und Aufsätze 1925-62*, 1966, pp. 202 ff. Later E. Dinkler investigated the narrative (*op. cit.*, pp. 127 ff).

16. G. Baumbach, *Die Zeloten*, p. 24, asserts that the comparison of the Gospels (one armed disciple— several) does by no means speak in favor of Brandon's thesis, according to which the tradition developed in the direction of viewing Jesus and his disciples as pacifistic, and hence sought to conceal their Zealotist tendencies.

17. *Das Messiasgeheimnis in den Evangelien*, 1901, 1913 (2nd ed.).

18. See the references in A. Merx, *Das Evangelium Matthaeus nach der syrischen im Sinaikloster gefun-*

denen Palimsesthandschrift, vol. II/1 of the total work, *Die vier kanonischen Evangelien nach ihren ältesten bekannten Texte,* 1902, pp. 382-84. Origen, in his *Commentary on Matthew* (Migne, *Patrologia Graeca* 13, 1757), writes expressly that Jesus' answer is neither positive nor negative.

19. See, e.g., E. Lohmeyer, *Das Evangelium des Markus,* 1937, pp. 232 f., and P. Winter, *On the Trial of Jesus,* pp. 142 f.

20. A. Schweitzer, *Die Mystik des Apostels Paulus,* 1930, p. 505; M. Dibelius, "Rom und die Christen im 1. Jahrhundert," in *Botschaft und Geschichte, Gesammelte Aufsätze,* vol. 2, 1956; and G. Bornkamm, *op. cit.,* p. 112, also correctly accept here an "ironical parallelism." G. Bornkamm, *op. cit.,* pp. 113 f., makes the very good concluding remark that the saying takes a position "against all attempts . . . whether they be revolutionary or conservative-loyalist, to try to aid the world with ideologies."

21. The explanations suggested in the course of centuries are so numerous and diverse that it would be worthwhile to write a history of the exegesis of this saying.

22. The same is no doubt to be said of the parallel Lucan saying (Luke 12:49) about the "fire" which Jesus has come to cast upon the earth. Our attention is here directed to Jesus' death.

23. See R. Bultmann and others, including G. Baumbach, *Die Zeloten,* pp. 23 f.

24. According to Josephus (*Bellum Judaicum* II.8.4) the Essenes always set out armed.

25. S. G. F. Brandon, *op. cit.,* pp. 208 ff., contests this tradition reproduced by Eusebius (*Historia Ecclesias-*

tica III.5.3), but in my opinion unsuccessfully. M. Hengel, in his theses referred to in n. 7 of this chapter, points out moreover that the Romans did not proceed against the disciples of Jesus until the persecution under Nero.

5   CONCLUDING REMARKS

1. According to Josephus, the Zealots represented the extreme wing of the Pharisaic movement.

APPENDIX

WHO WERE THE ZEALOTS?[*]

The Zealous were ardent defenders of the Law and of the natural life of the Jewish people. They opposed with relentless rigor any attempt to bring Judea under the dominion of idolatrous Rome, and were an aggressive and fanatical war party from the time of Herod until the fall of Jerusalem and Masada. The members of this party bore also the name *Sicarii*, from their custom of going about with daggers (*sicae*) hidden beneath their cloaks, with which they would stab anyone found committing a sacrilegious act or anything provoking anti-Jewish feeling.

Originally the name "Zealots" signified religious fanatics. Unfailing "zeal for the Law" became the standard of piety in the days of the Maccabean struggle against the Hellenizers. The Zealots of the Maccabean time were strict supporters of rabbinical laws governing the relations of Jews to idolators and idols. The divine attribute—"a jealous God"—is significantly explained as denoting that, while God is merciful and forgiving in regard to every other transgression, He exacts vengeance in the case of idolatry: "As long as there is idolatry in the world, there is divine wrath."

Regarding the original Zealots, Hippolytus says the following:

[*] This material is an edited and revised version of the article on the Zealots by K. Kohler in *The Jewish Encyclopedia* (New York: Funk & Wagnalls, 1905).

Some observe a still more rigid practise in not han-
dling or looking at a coin bearing an image, saying
that one should neither carry nor look at nor fashion
any image; nor will they enter a city at the gate of
which statues are erected, since they consider it unlaw-
ful to walk under an image. Others threaten to slay
any uncircumcised Gentile who listens to a discourse
on God and His laws, unless he undergoes the rite
of circumcision; should he refuse to do so, they kill
him instantly. From this practise they have received
the name of "Zealots" or "Sicarii." Others again call
no one Lord except God, even though one should
torture or kill them.

It is only this last point which Josephus singles out
as the doctrine of the Zealots of his day in order to
give them the character of political extremists; the rest
he omits. But even here he misstates the facts. The
principle that God alone is King is essentially a religious one. It found expression in the older liturgy.
It was to be pronounced in the *Shema* twice a day.
As early as 63 B.C. the Pharisaic elders in the name
of the nation declared to Pompey that it was not be-
fitting for them to be ruled by a king, because the
form of government received from their forefathers
was that of subjection to the priests of the God they
worshiped. The kingship of God is indeed especially
accentuated in the Psalms of Solomon.

ORGANIZATION AS A POLITICAL PARTY

The reign of the Idumean Herod (Herod the Great,
37-4 B.C.) gave the impetus for the organization of the
Zealots as a political party. Shemaiah and Abtalion,
as members of the Sanhedrin, at first opposed Herod,
but seem to have preferred a passive resignation in
the end; though there were those who "could by no

torments be forced to call him (Herod) king," and who persisted in opposing his government. Hezekiah and his so-called "band of robbers" who were the first to fall as victims under Herod's bloodthirsty rule were by no means common robbers. Josephus, following his sources, bestows the name of "robbers" upon all the ardent Jewish patriots who would not endure the reign of the usurper and who fled with their wives and children to the caves and fortresses of Galilee to fight and to die for their conviction and their freedom. All these "robbers" were in reality Zealots. Josephus relates of one of them that he slew his wife and his seven sons rather than allow them to be slaves to the Idumean Herod.

THE SICARII

It was for the sake of punishing the crimes of idolatry and bloodshed committed by Herod that the Zealots of Jerusalem first appeared with daggers (*sicae*) hidden underneath their cloaks, bent upon slaying the Idumean despot. Josephus relates that it was the introduction of Roman institutions entirely antagonistic to the spirit of Judaism, such as the gymnasium, the arena, and, above all, the trophies (that is, images to which homage was to be paid), which provoked the indignation of the people. Ten citizens of Jerusalem swore vengeance against Herod as an enemy of the nation, and, with concealed daggers, went into the theater, where Herod was supposed to be, in order to slay him. Owing, however, to his system of espionage, Herod was informed of the conspiracy in time, and so escaped, while the conspirators suffered death with great torture, but gloried in their martyrdom. The people sympathized with them, and in their wrath tore to pieces the spy who had discovered the plot. Another outburst of indignation on the part of the Zealots occurred when Herod, toward the end of his life, placed a large golden eagle over the great gate of the Temple. Two masters of the Law, Judah ben Sarifai and Mattathias ben Margalot, exhorted their disciples to sacrifice their lives rather than allow this violation of the Mosaic law, which forbids as idolatry the use of such images; and forty young men with these two teachers at their head pulled down the golden eagle, for which act the entire company suffered the cruel penalty of death by fire inflicted by order of Herod.

JUDAS, THE ZEALOT LEADER

The spirit of this Zealot movement, however, was not crushed. No sooner had Herod died (4 B.C.) than the people cried out for revenge and gave his son and successor Archelaus no peace. Judea was full of robber bands, says Josephus, the leaders of which each desired to be a king. It was then that Judas, the son of Hezekiah, the above-mentioned robber-captain, organized his forces for revolt, first, it seems, against the Herodian dynasty, and then, when Quirinius introduced the census, against submission to the rule of Rome and its taxation. Little reliance, however, can be placed upon Josephus regarding the character of Judas: at one point this author describes him as a leader "desirous only of the royal title" and bent upon "pillaging and destroying people's property" with the aid of "a multitude of men of profligate character"; elsewhere he mentioned Judas as "the founder of the

fourth sect of Jewish philosophy, who taught that God
is the only Ruler and Lord, and neither death nor any
dread should make them call any man Lord"; and at
the same time he says, "The nation was infected with
their doctrine to an incredible degree, which became
the cause of its many misfortunes, the robberies and
murders committed."

It was under the leadership of Judas and of his
sons and grandson that the Zealots became an aggressive and relentless political party which would brook
no compromise and would have no peace with Rome.
They were those who would bring about "the kingdom
of heaven," that is, the kingship of God, "by force
and violence" (Matt. 11:12). Of Judas' three sons,
Jacob and Simon fell as martyrs to their cause in opposing the Roman rule under Tiberius Alexander, his
other son, Menahem, was the chief leader of the revolt in 66, and was slain on account of his tyranny
by rivals in his own party when, surrounded with royal
pomp, he went up to the Temple to be crowned. His
kinsman and successor at Masada was the Zealot leader
Eleazar ben Jair. In the speech attributed to him he
declared that it is a glorious privilege to die for the
principle that none but God is the true Ruler of man-
kind, and that rather than yield to Rome, which is
slavery, men should slay their wives and children and
themselves, since their souls will live forever. This is
certainly not the language and conduct of the leader of
a band of "robbers," as Josephus persists in calling
this party. In their opposition to Rome the Zealots
were clearly inspired by religious motives.

As stated by Josephus, they boastfully called themselves by the name of *Kanna'im* (Zealots) on account
of their religious zeal. The right of the *Kanna'im* to

assassinate any non-Jew who dared to enter the consecrated parts of the Temple was officially recognized in a statute inscribed upon the Temple wall and discovered by Clermont-Ganneau in 1871. *Kanna'im* was the name for those zealous for the honor and sanctity of the Law as well as of the sanctuary, and for this reason they at first met with the support and encouragement of the people and of the Pharisaic leaders, particularly those of the rigid school of Shammai. It was only after they had been so carried away by their fanatic zeal as to become wanton destroyers of life and property throughout the land that they were denounced as heretic Galileans and "murderers" and that their principles were repudiated by the peace-loving Pharisees.

THEIR HISTORY

When in the year 5 Judas of Gamala in Galilee started his organized opposition to Rome, he was joined by one of the leaders of the Pharisees, R. Zadok, a disciple of Shammai and one of the fiery patriots and popular heroes who lived to witness the tragic end of Jerusalem. The taking of the census by Quirinius, the Roman procurator, for the purpose of taxation was regarded as a sign of Roman enslavement; and the Zealots' call for stubborn resistance to the oppressor was responded to enthusiastically. The anti-Roman spirit of the Zealots found its echo chiefly in the school of Shammai, who members did not shrink from resorting to the sword as the ultimate authority in matters of the Law when anti-heathen measures were to be adopted. A great many of the laws that are so strikingly hostile to idols and idolaters appear to have emanated from these times of warfare against Rome.

The call for political activity was renewed with greater force when, after the death of Agrippa I in the year 44, Judea became more emphatically a province of Rome and the Sanhedrin at Jerusalem was again deprived of its jurisdiction. Numerous bands of Zealots roamed through the land, fanning local strifes into wars of rebellion; but in every case they were ultimately defeated, and their leaders were either beheaded or banished for a time. Soon afterward Jacob and Simon, sons of Judas the Galilean, organized a revolt against Tiberius Alexander, and paid the penalty of crucifixion (47). But matters reached a climax under the procurators Cumanus, Felix, and Florus (49-64), who vied with one another in bloodthirsty cruelty and tyranny when the Zealot leaders, in their desperate struggle against the overwhelming power of an implacable enemy, resorted to extreme measures in order to force the people to action.

Three men are singled out by Josephus and in rabbinical tradition as having shown boundless ferocity in their warfare against Rome and Romanizers: Eleazar ben Dinai, Amram and Tahina. Of Eleazar ben Dinai and Amram it is said that "they desired to urge the Messianic deliverance of Israel, but fell in the attempt." Regarding Eleazar ben Dinai and Tahina, R. Johanan b. Zakkai relates that, on account of the frequent murders committed by them and which won them the epithet of "murderers," the Mosaic law concerning expiation for unknown slain ones was set in abeyance. Their dealings with property, especially that belonging to those suspected of friendliness to Rome, created anarchy throughout the land.

As the oppression of the Roman procurators increased, so also the passion and violence of the Zealots grew in intensity, affecting all the discontented, while one pseudo-Messiah after another appeared, arousing the hope of the people for deliverance from the Roman yoke. It was quite natural that under the name of *Sicarii* all kinds of corrupt elements, men eager for pillage and murder, should join the party, spreading terror through the land. Finally the barbarities of Albinus and, above all, of Gessius Florus precipitated the crisis and played into the hands of the terrorists (14-15). The issue was between the peace party, which was willing to yield to cruel Rome, and the war party, which while relying on God's help, demanded bold action; and under the leadership of the priestly governor of the Temple, Eleazar ben Anania, who refused to receive gifts from or offer sacrifice on behalf of Rome, the latter party prevailed. At this opportune time Menahem, the son of Judas, the Galilean, seized the fortress Masada in Galilee, killed the Roman garrison, and then drove the Romans out of other fortresses; and finally his kinsman and successor as master of Masada, Eleazar ben Jair, took up the war of rebellion against Rome and carried it to the very end.

True to the Shammaite principle that warfare against the heathen possessors of Palestine is permitted even on the Sabbath, the war was carried on by the Zealots on that day and the Romans were everywhere overpowered and annihilated, Simon bar Giora being one of the heroic leaders whom none could resist. The whole army of Cestius, who had brought twelve legions from Antioch to retrieve the defeat of the Roman garrison, was annihilated by Zealots under the leadership of Bar Giora and Eleazar ben Simon the priest. The Maccabean days seemed to have returned; and the patriots of Jerusalem celebrated the year 66 as the year of Israel's deliverance from Rome, and commemorated it with coins bearing the names of Eleazar the priest and Simon the prince.

The news of the victory of the Zealots in Jerusalem set the whole province of Galilee ablaze. Always a hotbed of revolution, it at once began an insurrection, and its thousands soon rallied round the fiery Zealot leaders. Only Sepphoris, a city full of aliens, obstinately refused to join the revolution. Josephus was sent by the Jerusalem Sanhedrin, composed chiefly of Zealots, for the purpose of prevailing upon the Sepphorites to abandon the cause of Agrippa II, and Rome, and to help Galilee work hand in hand with the authorities at Jesusalem in the liberation of Judea; but he deceived the Zealots and played into the hands first of Agrippa and then of Rome. His *De Bello Judaico* and his *Vita,* written for the purpose of pleasing his Roman masters, are full of aspersions upon the character of the Zealots and their leaders.

The year 67 saw the beginning of the great war with the Roman legions, first under Vespasian and then under Titus; and Galilee was at the outset chosen as the seat of war. The Zealots fought with almost superhuman powers against warriors trained in countless battles waged in all parts of the known world, and when they succumbed to superior military skill and overwhelming numbers, often only after some act of treachery within the Jewish camp, they died with a fortitude and a spirit of heroic martyrdom which amazed and overawed their victors. Josephus' own description of the tragic end of the last great Zealot leader, Eleazar ben Jair, and his men after the siege and final capture of Masada is the best refutation of his malicious charges against them.

At the siege of Jerusalem the Zealots were not de-

terred even by the defeat in Galilee and the terrible
massacre of their compatriots; their faith in the final
victory of the Holy City and its massive walls remained unshaken. But there were too much enmity and
strife between them and the ruling body, the Sanhedrin, which they distrusted; and their own leaders were
also divided. Instead of working after the clearly
mapped-out plan of one powerful leader, they had
their forces split up into sections. In order to force
the wealthy and more peaceably inclined citizens to
action, the Zealots in their fury set fire to the store-
houses containing the corn needed for the support of
the people during the siege. This tragic event is recorded in the only Talmudical passage that mentions
the *Kanna'im* as a political party.

Simon bar Giora and John of Giscala survived the
fall of Jerusalem, and were taken as captives to Rome
to glorify Titus' triumph; the former, with a rope
around his head, was dragged to the Forum and cast
down from the Tarpeian rock. Most of the Zealots
fell under the sword or other instrunments of death
and torture at the hands of the Romans, and such as
fled to Alexandria or Cyrenaica roused by their un-
yielding hostility to Rome the opposition of those
eager for peace, until they too finally met the same
tragic fate. It was a desperate and mad spirit of de-
fiance which animated them all and made them prefer
horrible torture and death to Roman servitude. History
has declared itself in favor of the Pharisees, who
deemed the schoolhouse of more vital importance to
the Jews than state and Temple; but the Zealot, too,
deserves due recognition for his sublime type of stead-
fastness.

INDEX OF AUTHORS

INDEX OF BIBLICAL REFERENCES

84

70 71 72 73 10 9 8 7 6 5 4 3 2 1

ST. MARY'S COLLEGE OF MARYLAND
ST. MARY'S CITY, MARYLAND

42007